RYE IN PICTURES

Today, Rye's ancient character is justifiably one of the jewels of the South-East of England if not the country.

It is a town for strolling the many cobbled streets with their proud medieval, Tudor, Stuart and Georgian houses, great pubs, a fine church and all the ancient landmarks that make up this unique town.

A Little History

A thousand years ago, Rye was likely to have been an island sitting close to the mouth of the Appledore Estuary and home to a small fishing village that did not warrant an entry in the Domesday Book of 1086.

The 12th century established Rye as a borough, King Stephen founded a mint during his reign (1135-54) and Rye developed a fishing industry that would continue until the present day.

In the 14th century, both Rye and Winchelsea became '**Antient Towns'**, limbs under the head Cinque Port of Hastings. *Cinque Ports - a confederation with privileges including the right to land and sell fish at Yarmouth in exchange for the requirement to provide 2 ships each for the king's service, out of the total of 20 required from Hastings. (Cinque is pronounced as 'sink' rather than the French 'sank')*

Over the next two hundred years, Rye would grow in importance to become the largest and most prosperous town in Sussex, home to 1200 tons of shipping with fishing and cargo boats sailing in on the flood tide.

The streets would have bustled with merchants and sailors and later with pirates and smugglers involved in what was considered to be a 'noble trade' that contributed greatly to the town's economy.

That the charm of medieval Rye survived to this day can be attributed largely to its lack of access to a road network and its isolation on the Sussex coast. Most of its visitors arrived by sea and entered the town through the Strandgate.

By the time that the Turnpike roads arrived in the late 18th century and the railway in 1851, Rye's charms within its citadel were secure.

The unique medieval streets, for so long ignored and side lined, were now linked to the outside world and they soon came to the e   inspiration. Such creative circles included th and Radclyffe Hall and the painters Paul Nas

'Motor tourists' now filled the many hotels to by Rye's red roofs. Tourism was born, fuelled special and it continues to this day.

GU00697197

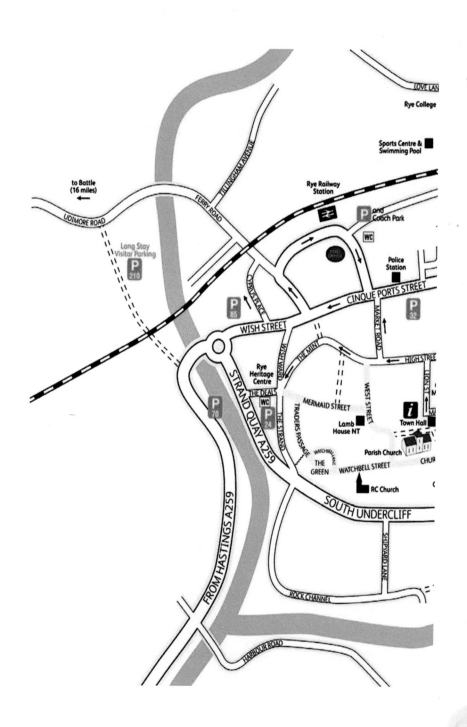

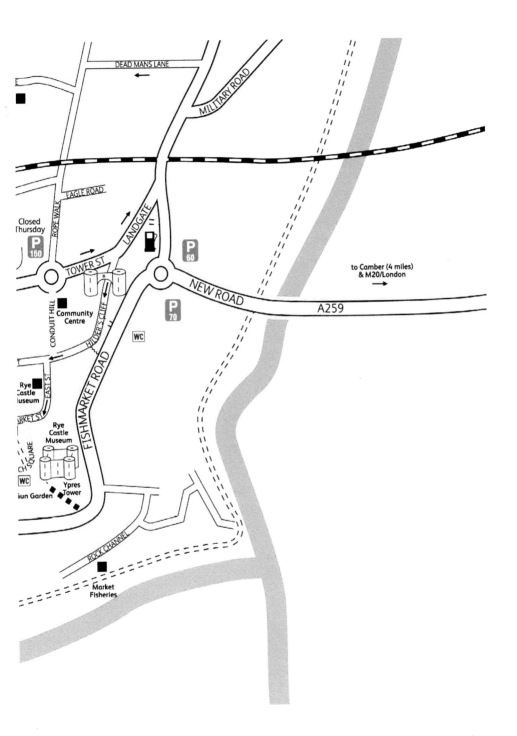

The Strand Quay

Boatbuilding and commerce have been the backbone of Rye since medieval times. Then the Tillingham river was wider and its banks lined with boats all waiting to be unloaded into the black, weather boarded warehouses right up to the 1950s.

The docks finally closed when the A259 was re-routed by the side of the river creating today's Strand Quay.

Rye Heritage Centre stands on the corner of the Strand Quay and The Deals and a visit to the beautifully crafted town model brings seven hundred years of the town's rich history to life in its 'Story of Rye'. The old net shops and warehouses have become antique shops, restaurants, cafes and the wharf now moorings for yachts.

Games of Pétanque are played out on the quay before retiring, for a post-match tipple, to The Ship with its list of Revenue Cutters and ships of the Coastal Blockade

on the wall. Lord Pembroke's quote reflects the power of the smugglers.

Dating from 1592, The Ship was once a warehouse at a time when Rye was at its height. Later, it became a Customs Warehouse for confiscated contraband sold at auction to the highest bidder. The custom of 'tasting the goods before buying' led at first to an *ad hoc* bar, a pub by 1722 and a fully licensed inn by 1836.

Almost everybody who visited Rye would come by sea and land at the Strand Quay, the safest moorings between the Thames and The Solent, amidst the hustle and bustle and noise of the dock. Traders, sailors, dockers and porters and carters would all make their entry into Rye through the Strand Gate, Rye's gateway to the world, and walk up 'Middle Street' (*now Mermaid Street*) to the top of the hill and the centre of the town, the pubs, inns and shops eager to relieve them of their money.

The Strand Gate was one of Rye's four gates, it stood next to the *Blew Anchor* until the gate was demolished in about 1815 and widened the access for all the carts and wagons taking goods to and from the harbour.

The Blew Anchor remained popular for 300 years but, despite its change of name in 1897, to The Borough Arms, trade began to wane. By 1907 the old pub was sold at auction and became housing and later a B&B. What are now the tea rooms was once the pub's tap room and after the sale became a Customs Office and then a Labour Office, finding work in the warehouses and on the quays during the Depression - on the wall is a plaque to the Strand Gate. *(photograph courtesy of the Old Borough Arms)*

Mermaid Street

Once the main road into the centre of town, Mermaid Street still links the Strand Quay to the Citadel.

The houses that line its cobbles reflect the glory of the 15th, 16th and 17th centuries with Hartshorn House (right) and Jeake's House (below) just two of the many that catch the eye.

Samuel Jeake (II) was a merchant, a diarist, a non-conformist and was made a Freeman of Rye the year after Jeake's House was built in 1690.

The gabled Hartshorn House was given to Samuel Jeake as part of the dowry of the young Elizabeth Hartshorn whom he married in1681. During the Napoleonic Wars it became a hospital and for many years after was known as 'The Old Hospital'. The blue plaque bears witness to the American poet, novelist and critic Conrad Aiken who bought Jeake's House for £1700 in January 1924.

Today Mermaid Street is full of novelty, reflected in the names of houses such as 'The House Opposite' *(so called as the owners were fed up with being asked directions to The Mermaid Inn)* and the House with Two Front Doors *(rather obvious again)* but the history of Mermaid Street was less than reputable.

The rich and the poor lived cheek by jowl, the inns and boarding houses catered for the many 'needs' of the traders and sailors 'carousing' up from the port.

In the 1740s The Mermaid Inn was synonymous with the Hawkhurst Gang. Ruthless and violent, they made it their headquarters until the gang's demise in 1748.

Sitting by the window, it is easy to imagine those dark times with guns lying on the table and brandy, gin and tea hidden in the cellars.

First built over a vaulted 13th century cellar, the Mermaid's timber framed, latticed windows and galleries date from the 16th century. By 1770, the inn was in decline and became tenements for the poor and a workhouse - it would not begin to resume its importance, as one of Rye's premier hostelries, until the beginning of the 20th century.

The floors still creak and the ghosts still haunt the rooms of one of Rye's most photographed inns.

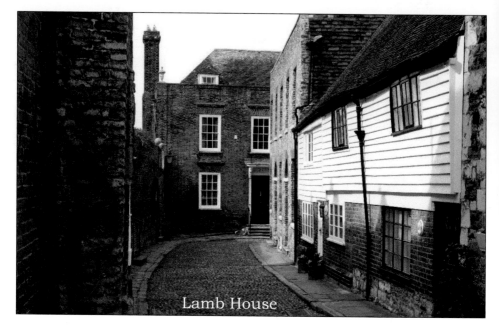
Lamb House

No visit to Rye would be complete without a tour of Lamb House that dates from 1722 and built at the behest of James Lamb, a wealthy wine merchant. It would be the beginning of a dynasty that would last for 250 years for this, the pre-eminent family of Rye.

From a tablet in Rye Church, James Lamb was said to *be "a man of uncommen virtue who with the integrity of a merchant and the courtesy of a gent united the undissembled piety of a true christian. His distinguishing abilities raised him no less than 13 times to the Mayoralty of this corporation, which office he always filled with dignity that shewed him born for precedence"* although this statement fails to acknowledge his link to the infamous John Breads and the *'Murder most Foul'* that would shock Rye in 1743.

The symmetry of Lamb House would become the home of such literary giants as Henry James, EF Benson and Rumer Godden with their equally famous visitors. EF Benson in particular, immortalised Rye as *Tilling* in his stories of *Mapp and Lucia* and for aficionados there is much to connect fact with fiction.

Sadly, the Garden Room, where Elizabeth Mapp would sit and watch those of importance on their way to play golf, shop or on Sundays, walk to church is no more but the streets and views have not changed in 90 years.

St Mary the Virgin

Rye's Parish Church, built in 1103, dominates the skyline and the surrounding countryside from its position on the highest point of the citadel and is woven into Rye's folklore. Despite the best efforts of the French, some of the original building remains. Today it is a 'Heinz 57' mixture of Norman, Transitional, Early English, Decorated and Modern.

At the mid-point in the 100 Years War when the French had succeeded in gaining control of the Channel, raiding parties attacked towns all along the south coast. In 1377, Rye was looted, the town, set on fire and the church was so badly damaged that the roof fell in and, even worse, the French stole the church bells and took them back to France.

The next year, 'Ryers' sailed across the Channel to wreak similar havoc upon the towns of St Pierre-en-Porte and Veulettes. They took back what the French had taken the previous year and recovered the church bells and the lead that had been stripped from the church. Hostages were taken for ransom and St Pierre was set on fire. On their return to Rye, one of the bells was hung in the town to give a warning of any future attack and the street became known as Watchbell Street. The bell on The Green is a replica.

The church was soon rebuilt and re-roofed for worship. A 'new' clock, made by the Huguenot Lewys Billiard of Winchelsea, was added in the 1560s. This church turret clock still works, one of the oldest in the country and the pendulum that was added later swings inside the church. There are some fine stained glass windows, an 18th century carved mahogany altar, a candelabrum hanging in the chancel that dates from 1759 and the Rye Millennium Embroidery to muse over.

The famous 'Quarter Boys', that strike the quarters but not the hours, were added in 1760.

The church tower is worth the climb not just for the views but also for the 8 bells that hang there. Added in 1775, six of the original bells were recast with two new bells added.

Watchbell Street is typical of most streets in Rye. Lined with Grade I and Grade II listed properties with many dating from the 16th century or even earlier although some were re-fronted in the 18th century.

It is a quiet street now with perhaps 50 people living in the houses between the Hope Anchor and the Ypres Tower, but it was not always so.

In the 16th and 17th centuries, the rich and poor lived side by side and again in the 19th century.

Some were high officials but many had jobs linked to the sea and the smell of fish drying was not to everyone's taste.

The women were likely to be servants, cleaners, laundresses, dressmakers, straw bonnet makers or shrimp sellers. Later, there would be schoolmistresses, governesses and 'companions' and of course ladies.

In the 19th century, Town Clerks, Clerks of the Peace, Justices of the Peace and other important men lived 'next door' to fishermen, labourers, carpenters, blacksmiths and bootmakers, 285 people of all classes, a mix of generations and relatives and a third were children. (Rye Castle Museum)

The small but beautifully formed white painted Franciscan Catholic Church, dedicated to St Anthony of Padua, would not shine its light on Watchbell Street until 1929.

The rich stained glass windows and the marbled interior provide the perfect place for contemplation for those who enter in and to admire the rood cross, the gift of the author Radclyffe Hall who lived in Rye.

Church Square from the Church

St Anthony's

Watchbell Street becomes Church Square. On the corner is St Anthony of Padua, 15th century timber framed house that was once the home of the Sedley family in the early 20th century. Frederick Sedley was a benefactor of the Franciscan order and of the church in Watchbell Street.

The beauty of today's view of cobbled streets and old houses is at odds with what it must have been like 150 years ago and Hucksteps Row would have been typical.

A narrow small alley that in 1841 would have led to 17 houses in which 80 people lived, half of them children.

For both Church Square and Watchbell Street, the town pump provided their water and until 1880, there was little indoor sanitation. There were a few gas streetlights from 1846 but inside, candles and oil lamps would have been used for lighting well into the 1930s. Today there are 6 houses in Hucksteps Row and fewer than 10 residents.

Ypres Tower

There were designs for a grand castle, linked to the town wall, to defend against the French, but by 1250 only the tower had been built. The Town Fort survived the burning of Rye in 1377 but, before the end of the 100 Years' War with France (*1453*), it was considered to be of no further use and sold to one John de Ypres as a private house! By the late 15th century, it became the town's prison until downgraded to the status of a lock-up by the Prison Act of 1865 which it remained until 1891. It is now Rye Castle Museum with stories of smuggling and Captain Pugwash whose author John Ryan lived just a few yards away, the macabre gibbet of John Breads and great views across the marsh from the top of the tower.

Through the arch into the Gun Garden *'furnished with greate ordinance'* in 1587, the year before the Spanish Armada sailed up the Channel and threatened Rye, but the cannon were never fired in anger. By 1649 it had become a bowling green but in 1740, the gun platform was strengthened and expanded again to counter further threats from the French.

By 1925 it was a public viewpoint and any military ambition now limited to our or our children's imagination.

With the sea lapping at the cliff the threat of attack was very real but the sea has retreated, the river re-routed and the marsh is largely dry. In the distance is Dungeness, south is Rye Harbour and to the east, the forest of windmills bring animation to Romney Marsh.

n Salts

by the Ypres Castle Inn lead to the
nd to what was once the
pedestrian gate and one of
Rye but the gate was
in the mid-14th century.

the road are perhaps a
alt-houses, round and
ecame known as Rye,
omesday entry for

orm of 1287, rudimentary
Rye from the high tides
breached the riverbanks. To
protection and the maintenance
waterways a tax, called a "scot", was
enforced. The people who lived on higher ground, away from the threat from
flooding, were exempt from paying this tax and got off 'scot free', a phrase we still
use today.

Once, the Town Wall and the cliff, would have formed a formidable defensive line
when the sea lapped at the cliff but it did little to stop those marauding French of
1377 when sacking and burning the town.

The Saltings were enclosed in 1834, an embankment stopped the flooding of the
Town and Middle Salts and by 1897, they were established as the town's recreation
ground and cricket pitch and now they present a different view of Rye.

The Landgate guards the north entrance to Rye and the London Road. Then, Rye was almost surrounded by the sea with the only access at high tide by the 'Landgate'. Built in 1329, it did little to guard against the devastating French attack of 1377.

The massive round towers stand 40' high and were once topped with a projecting parapet (*the supporting gables can still be seen*) where stones or boiling water could be dropped on any attackers. The grooves for the portcullis are etched in the side walls, but the arrow slits are now home to pigeons.

Hilders Cliff leads to The Lookout where in 1287, you would have seen the world change as in some disaster movie. Great storms, huge waves, the sound of the wind and the shingle, endless days and nights and at the end, Winchelsea was destroyed, the shingle had moved to create new rivers and the coastline began to recede from Rye and Romney. It was almost apocalyptic in its fury. At low tide, the marsh was revealed and Rye would no longer be an island town.

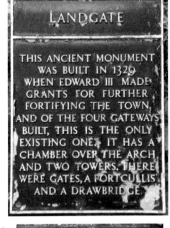

LANDGATE

THIS ANCIENT MONUMENT WAS BUILT IN 1329 WHEN EDWARD III MADE GRANTS FOR FURTHER FORTIFYING THE TOWN, AND OF THE FOUR GATEWAYS BUILT, THIS IS THE ONLY EXISTING ONE. IT HAS A CHAMBER OVER THE ARCH AND TWO TOWERS. THERE WERE GATES, A PORTCULLIS AND A DRAWBRIDGE.

THIS LOOKOUT WAS GIVEN IN 1935 BY E.F. BENSON WHEN MAYOR OF RYE. HE IMMORTALISED THIS TOWN AS "TILLING" IN HIS MAPP AND LUCIA NOVELS.

High Street

The blue plaque at Number 4 remembers 'Radclyffe Hall poet and author', whose lesbian novel 'The Well of Loneliness' was banned for over 20 years as a 'danger to the nation' - it has since become a modern classic. It was the same Radclyffe that donated the [illegible] to the Church of St Anthony of Padua on [illegible] Street.

The Old Apothecary Shop on the corner dates from 1777 and is now a coffee house with many of the original drawers and fittings inside. Dry ingredients would have been ground together with sugar and water for making syrups or with alcohol for tinctures.

At 1 High Street, Dial House is synonymous with Gills Clockmakers who traded from the late 17th to the late 18th centuries. They are most likely to have made Rye's two 'Parliamentary Clocks', one at the Town Hall and one that takes pride of place in The George and survived the disastrous fire of 2019.

The "George" was Rye's Oldest Coaching Inn and Gills' Parliament clock now hangs on the wall by the bar. As they say, it kept the right time twice a day!

Opposite Lion Street, the large red br[ick h]ouse built in 1636 and flanked by two ancient oak doors, is noted for its brickwork and its dormer windows that are amongst the earliest of their type in England.

First it was the home of the Jurat (*magistrate*) Thomas Peacocke and on his death in 1638, the building became a Free School for Boys that lasted until 1907 when a new school was opened in The Grove.

Lion Street leads up the hill to St Mary's Church, the Town Hall and Market Street, once the site of the medieval market.

Lined with shops and restaurants, there are eight Grade II listed buildings, two of which date from the 16th century and the rest from the 18th century.

At the very top, close to the church door is Fletcher's House, a 16th-century timber-framed house with continuous jetties on three sides that overlooked the street on the east and the former market lanes on the south and north.

John Fletcher (b:1579) was the son of a curate of Rye (later to became Bishop of London and Chaplain to Queen Elizabeth I). John was a playwright who collaborated with Shakespeare on *Henry VIII* and *The Two Noble Kinsmen*.

Shakespeare came to Rye with his touring company 1597 and performed at the Mermaid Inn.

was an important place.

Market Street

The Town Hall (*built 1743*) dominates, crowned with cupolas and with a market arcade below. Under its charter of 1289, Rye was an independent borough granted rights of governance, with its own mayor and magistrates (*the Jurats*) and the Jurats' Bell is still rung to summon the Quarter Sessions.

Opposite the Town Hall and next door to the shop on the corner, was the town's old bakery, with its uneven roofs and dormer windows, and thought to date from the late 1300s.

It was known as 'Ye Olde Tuck Shoppe' but of more interest is the chimney of the bakehouse that had a pulley at the top to haul kegs of smuggled brandy up to the attics above – surely every home should have one and perhaps they do in Rye!

Further down Market Street, at the corner with East Street, lived Paul Nash the acclaimed painter and his painting of Rye Harbour hangs in the Ferens Art Gallery, Hull.

In the 1930s, he was part of Rye's artistic and literary circle that included Radclyffe Hall, Conrad Aiken, E F Benson and Edward Burra.

The black and white house named Flushing, on the corner of Church Passage and Market Square, was once an 18th century inn but the frescos found inside suggest it to be at least 450 years old but, there is a more sinister history.

In 1736, the .... John Breads (*Breeds*) owned the Flushing Inn. A friend of smugglers, Breads was .... on the edge of what was .... and was fined by the Mayor, John Lamb, for giving 'short weight'.

Breads waited seven years for his revenge and on one Friday night in March 17.. Mayor Lamb was due to have dinner with his son John aboard the revenue sl.. anchored at the Fishmarket Quay.

Too ill to attend Lamb asked his brother-in-law, Allen Grebell, to go in his place and with little time to spare Allen took Lamb's cloak for the evening. Everyone in Rye knew of the Lamb's celebration but not of the substitution.

Later, Grebell, climbed the steps by the Ypres Castle Inn and as he crossed the graveyard to return home, Breads, armed with a large knife, stabbed him twice in the back.

Grebell staggered home and told his manservant that 'a drunken man had knocked into him'. He sat down by the fire and in the morning, was found dead, still wearing the mayoral cloak.

There probably have been more cleverer murderers then Breads, who not only dropped his initialled blood-stained knife in the churchyard, but in his drunken state he had staggered around Rye shouting 'Butchers should kill Lambs'.

Arrested and sentenced to death, on 8th June 1743, Breads was hanged just outside the Strand Gate.

The next day, the body was encased in a metal cage and hung from a gibbet in a field, now known as Gibbets Marsh, by the windmill.

The cell where Breads was held can be found in the Ypres Tower together with the grisly replica of the cage complete with its fake skeleton – at least I think it is!

Church Passage East *(formerly Pump Street)*

Water was important for Rye and in the 16th century, money was set aside for the repair of the town's water supply. A cistern was built in 1520, probably on the Strand and a second, in 1548, in the churchyard that was renewed in 1735 and can be seen today. The cistern is oval, measures 30 feet by 20 feet and holds 20,000 gallons of water, enough for those packed 18th century streets. The lead pump was added in 1826.

The water was taken from springs, that ran to the foot of Conduit Hill and was then pumped along 2" elm pipes up the cobbled hill to the Water Cistern by the church. It is said that two donkeys provided the power for the pump. In 1869, as demand for water increased, a Waterworks was built at the bottom of Conduit Hill, a steam engine and pump were installed and the donkeys finally 'retired'.

The foot of Conduit Hill was also close to the medieval pedestrian Postern Gate that was removed in 1819, the same year that the Strandgate was demolished.

Conduit Hill

Conduit Hill

In 1379, on land to the east of Conduit Hill, Augustinian Friars were granted permission to build a new Friary following the disastrous French raid of 1377. Their former 'monastery' was destroyed by fire along with most of Rye.

The Monastery was suppressed i 1538 and passed into ~~ hands. Over the years most ~ buildings have been demolished. and the stone used elsewhere in Rye, but the Chapel and the steps have remained as a constant in Rye's history for almost 650 years but not without its scandal.

Soon after the new Monastery was built, one of the monks fell in love with a Rye girl and would not give her up, breaking his vow of celibacy. Sentenced to death, the two lovers were both bricked up in a cell by the northern wall and their cries, as they went mad, gave Turkey Cock Lane its name. In 1845, it is said that two skeletons were discovered in a bricked-up wall, still clasped in each other's arms!

At the bottom of Conduit Hill, Tower Street becomes Cinque Ports Street and behind the small car park on the left is one of the best examples of Rye's Town Wall. Begun in 1381 (four years after the disastrous French raid), it ran from the Land Gate to the Strand Gate and linked up with the steep cliff on the south of Rye on which stood the Castle (Ypres)Tower.

A section of wall, almost twenty feet in height, can also be seen on Wish Ward, behind the old Strand Conduit with its antiquated pump, and also in the ground floor passageway of the Old Borough Arms.

The Mint

In the 12th century, under Common Law, only boroughs had the right of coinage although it is believed that Rye was a Borough by the time King Stephen came to the throne.

.... King is said to have founded a mint at ..... during his reign (1135-54) although, officially, Rye did not receive its charter until 1289 during King Edward I's rule.

In The Mints Of Rye In The Reign Of Stephen, W. J. Andrew writes:

Rye supplied its own moneyer, Radulf, Rawulf or Raul, as he variously spells his name on the coins, and of his coinage we have to-day eight pennies and two (cut) halfpennies, from several different dies, which, therefore, indicate a considerable output from the mint. The obverses continue the same legend as before, but the reverses vary as + RADVLF : ON : RIE, + RAPVLF : ON : RIE, and + RAVL : ON : RIE, for Ralph of, or at, Rye.'

Despite the evidence, no Mint has been located and Mint Street, originally called Long Street, connected the Strand Gate to the Land Gate and was the only direct link through town within the town walls. The lower road, closer to the quay, was lined first with warehouses then shops and businesses, including The Forester's Arms, The Standard and The Swan that all date from the 1800s.

The Old Bell, a part of which is the oldest building on The Mint, has quite likely been an inn since the mid-15th century and later, the haunt of smugglers.

Hidden cupboards, revolving cupboards, 'tubby' holes, false walls and panels were all part of the fabric of *'The Olde Bell'*. A smugglers tunnel was dug from The Mermaid to The Bell and used to move their illegal goods away from the prying eyes of the Revenue.

Regrettably, the evidence of such a fascinating history has been destroyed in successive 'restorations' although the old beams and the vaulted cellar remain.

The Mint curves down to The Strand and connects to the former ancient harbour alongside the River Tillingham.

Before the railway and roads took the trade away, farmers shipped all their corn out by sea. One of the old corn stores was Stonham and Company, Agricultural Merchants who built the grand round windowed offices at the corner of The Deals and Wish Ward.

The grain stores were part of the black timbered buildings opposite.

The Strand still connects to the harbour and Rye Heritage Centre was formerly the warehouse of Hind's Woodyard.

The three-ton anchor that stands outside Rye Heritage Centre, dates from around 1530 and was likely to have been lost from a large "man o' war", probably by sailing too fast when lowering the anchor.

It was recovered from Rye Bay in 1993.

Rye's isolation, except by sea, began to change with the building of the Military Road, and the Royal Military Canal, at the beginning of the 19th century.

The later turnpikes and the railway of 1841 opened Rye to the outside world. Rye was unspoilt, attractive and fashionable and perfect for those seeking inspiration away from the capital. It was to the dawning of a literary and artistic age that would last well into the 20th century.

Some made Rye their home, some took short tenancies and others were visitors but all contributed to the aura of Rye. The homes of Henry James, Conrad Aiken, Radclyffe Hall and the painter Paul Nash are identified by their Blue Plaques. Rumer Godden lived at Lamb House after E. F. Benson, whose Mapp and Lucia stories of Tilling have immortalised Rye.

The fictitious Tilling landmarks can all be identified to those who have read the books and the modern reprint includes a map.

Traders Passage stretches from the bottom of Mermaid Street to Watchbell Street and leads to the Hope Anchor Inn. The Inn became 'The Trader's Arms' in Mapp and Lucia, where Lucia and Georgie spent their first night in Tilling in adjoining and **very** separate bedrooms.

Benson's view of Rye is one of subtle humour, mocking the residents and Edward Burra, the painter, referred to the town as 'Wry'!

Rye Harbour

With the decline of the Strand Quay, Rye's Harbour moved 1½ miles south along the River Rother with quays and warehousing built for bigger ships.

The view from the Gun Garden, along the river to the new harbour, was painted by surrealist Paul Nash in 1932.

"The Rye Marshes" marked the beginning of a radical new approach to landscape, flattened clouds, heavy sea and an angular river channel and the result is a severe and uncompromising abstract.

The original is in the Ferens Art Gallery, Hull but postcards of the painting can be bought almost anywhere in Rye.

The village of Rye Harbour also marks the start of the Rye Harbour Nature Reserve and its miles of walks along shingle ridges, salt marshes, lagoons and a wild and windswept coast.

Camber Castle

In 1514, a blockhouse was built on the coast to defend Rye and by 1540, it was greatly expanded into a castle as part of Henry VIII's network of coastal defences (the ... *Forts*) established ...wing the break from ...me to counter any potential ...

...stle had gained four outer bastions by 1543 but the vagaries of the weather ...ck again and as the sea retreated, the Castle was left high and dry a mile inland ...t of little use to the army or the navy. By 1637 it had been decommissioned and ...ll marooned for walkers to imagine what it must have been like in its pomp with ...nnon topping the rounded walls and a garrison of 42 men.

Royal Military Canal (RMC)

The RMC flows through by Rye. It was a massive undertaking, designed as a defence against Napoleon, but was not fully finished until 1809 some four years after the Battle of Trafalgar when the threat of invasion had passed. The canal runs for 28

miles from Cliff End (Pett Level) to Seabrook, near Folkestone and was designed to be 19 metres wide at the surface, 13.5 metres wide at the bottom and 3 metres deep. The excavated soil was piled on to the north bank to make a defensive parapet where the army could be positioned out of sight of the French.

The canal is 'kinked' with bends right and left at regular intervals that allowed a greater field of fire along the length of the canal, a clever concept that can still be seen. Behind the RMC, a Royal Military Road was built and, together with its bridges, were the first stage in better linking Rye to the outside world and are still in use today. In 1802, there were plans for a Weald of Kent Canal from the River Medway to Rye that would utilise the RMC for its final few miles to Rye but regretfully, the canal was never built. Now the RMC helps drain the marsh which is perhaps more relevant.

19th century Cottages,
Military Road

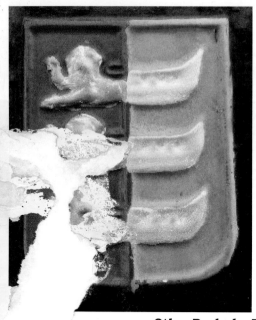

David Clarke has asserted his right under the Copyright, Designs and Patents Act 1998 to be identified as the author of this work.

Text, and photographs are

Copyright © David Clarke

1st July 2019.

All rights reserved.

No reproduction permitted without the prior consent of the author.

Published by History Walks,

St Leonards on Sea, East Sussex

This version dated 30th June 2022

ISBN: 978-1-9163083-5-0

Other Books by David Clarke

Long Distance Walks

1. Capital to Coast - 1066 Harold's Way
2. Walking the High Weald - Three Castles and an Ironmaster's House

Books

1. 1066 The Saxon Times
2. Rye in Pictures

Short Walks in 1066 Country

1. A Green St Leonards on Sea Walk
2. Walks around Battle (*Battle Circular Walks*)
3. 1066 Bodiam Castle to Battle Abbey
4. Walking Hastings to Rye, Rye to Hastings
5. Secret St Leonards Walking Trail
6. Pub Walks in Hastings and St Leonards
7. 1066 William's Way, Hastings to Battle
8. Rock a Nore to De La Warr
9. Pub Walks in 1066 Country
10. A Walk around Rye
11. A Walk around Winchelsea
12. More Walks around Rye